Civilization a

Reflections on Virtue and the Settlement of a New World

Rt. Rev. James D. Heiser
Bishop of the Evangelical Lutheran Diocese of North America

Repristination Press
Malone, Texas

DEDICATION

To my wife, Denise, and to my children, John and Anastasia, who share in the dream of expanding human civilization to a new world, and who—far more importantly—live in the confident hope of a new heavens and new earth in which righteousness dwells (2 Peter 3:13).

REPRISTINATION PRESS
P.O. BOX 173
BYNUM, TEXAS 76631

WWW.REPRISTINATIONPRESS.COM

ISBN 1-891469-48-7

Table of Contents

Introduction   5
I. What is a New Civilization Worth?   7
II. Virtue and the Settlement of a New World   21
III. Space Exploration and Christian Hope   39
IV. Faith and Community: Moving beyond LEO 57

Introduction

This is now the second volume of essays on the rather broad topic of the civilization and space travel which I have now had the privilege of setting before the public. My earlier volume, *A Shining City on a Higher Hill: Christianity and the Next New World* (2006) included essays spanning the years from the founding of the Mars Society in 1998 through the 2005 convention of that organization. (A paper I was privileged to present to the 2004 *Higher Things* youth conference of the Lutheran Church—Missouri Synod was also included in that earlier volume.)

Over the years since the release of *A Shining City*, members of the Mars Society have continued to offer very helpful insights regarding the interplay between theology and science. I greatly appreciate the many discussions which meetings of the Mars Society have afforded and hope I have given as much of a contribution to such dialog as I have received. And, that being said, and given my recent appointment to the Board of Directors of the Mars Society, I would observe that the contents of this small volume are my own thoughts, and should not be construed as in any way speaking on behalf of either the board, or the membership in general, of the Mars Society.

Rt. Rev. James D. Heiser
Festival of St. Michael and All Angels
29 September A.D. 2010

I. "What is a New Civilization Worth?"[1]

Abstract:
Why go to Mars? One of the main reasons is that Mars offers the hope of a new branch of civilization. But it is one thing to hope for a civilization, and another thing to build one. Civilizations are usually defined by a shared history, law, and other elements of culture, but a civilization is more than the sum of its parts. Healthy civilizations seek to embody common ideas and aspirations which claim a higher priority than the aspirations of individuals; civilizations are created by men and women but they seek to accomplish that which is beyond the abilities, or even the vision, of any individual member of such a civilization.

Walter M. Miller, Jr. (*Canticle for Leibowitz*) wrote a short story of the settlement of Mars, "Crucifixus Etiam," which asks the key question: "Which would you rather be: a sower or a reaper?" Reapers live off the civilizations built by others; sowers build new civilizations, often at great cost to themselves. Reapers think of themselves; sowers think of the generations to come. To plant a new civilization on Mars, we need to sow, so that others may someday reap.

•••••

Nine annual conferences devoted to discussing possibilities for exploring and possibly colonizing the Red Planet is an accomplishment of no small note. Nevertheless, this pales in significance when compared to the generations, even centuries, of discussions of humanity exploring the depths of space.[2] Lu-

---

[1] This essay was originally presented to the ninth annual international convention of the Mars Society, meeting in Washington, D.C. in August 2006.

[2] Already in the early 17th century, Johannes Kepler wrote to Galileo Galilei: "let us create vessels and and sails adapted to the heavenly ether." "There will be plenty of people unafraid of the empty void. In the meantime, we shall prepare, for the brave sky-travellers, maps of the celestial bodies—I shall do it for the moon, you, Galileo, for Jupiter. (Quoted in Noble 117)

minaries such as Johannes Kepler literally dreamed of space flight; and by 1638, Bishop John Wilkins, chief founder and first secretary of the Royal Society was openly speculating about the prospects of men setting forth into space after the fashion of the great explorers of the terrestrial globe:

> In the first ages of the world the Islanders either thought themselves to be the only dwellers upon the earth, or else if there were any other, yet they could not possibly conceive how they might have any commerce with them, being severed by the deep and broad Sea, but the after-times found out the invention of ships, in which notwithstanding none but some bold daring men durst venture, there being few so resolute as to commit themselves unto the vast Ocean, and yet now how easy a thing is this, even to a timorous and cowardly nature? So, perhaps, there may be some other means invented for a conveyance to the Moon, and though it may seem a terrible and impossible thing ever to pass through the vast spaces of the air, yet no question there would be some men who durst venture this as well as the other. True indeed, I cannot conceive any possible means for the like discovery of this conjecture, since there can be no sailing to the Moon, unless that were true which the Poets do but feign, that she made her bed in the Sea. We have not now any Drake or Columbus to undertake this voyage, or any Daedalus to invent a conveyance through the air. However, I doubt not but that time which is still the father of new truths, and hath revealed unto us many things which our Ancestors were ignorant of, will also manifest to our posterity, that which we now desire, but cannot know. (*A World in the Moon* 207–9)

The possibility of interplanetary colonization was already openly discussed in the seventeenth century, which Wilkins declaring, "Kepler doubts not, but that as soon as the art of flying is found out, some of their Nation will make one of the first colonies that shall inhabit that other world." (210)[3] Nearly four hundred years have passed, and such dreams still move us.

Naturally, enthusiasts wish that all of this would be far beyond the 'talking' phase; what they want are 'results.' But I believe that the 'talking' is a crucial part of the process; if we were ready, we would *do*, and not *talk*. I believe that on a deep level, we are not quite ready for this step, even now. We are still finding our path.

The delay is clearly not simply a matter of engineering; we have become quite adept at solving merely technical problems; the flight to the moon was accomplished in an astoundingly brief period of time when all that remained was the matter of the engineering. In 1609, Kepler wrote his famous *Somnium*, his dream of standing upon the moon. Three hundred and sixty years would pass from the *Somnium* to the Sea of Tranquility; this world was changed over and over again during those years—nations rose, mankind's knowledge of this world grew—until the time was right. Then, even the flimsiest of excuses—a 'Cold War' and the legacy of a politician—would suffice.

The central issues which continue to confront us are not fundamentally those of science or engineering; they are cultural. I realize that the Terrible Simplifiers seek to collapse all of humanity first into biology, and then, ultimately, subvert all of creation into mere subcategories of physics. The simplifiers are servants of ideology; and, as Russell Kirk declared, "if 'science' is converted into ideology, a substitute for philosophy and religion, then men of humane and social imagination will

---

[3] It is worth noting that such speculations did not interfere with Wilkins' rise to prominence in the Church and influence within the State.

recoil from the fraud." (63) Or in the words of philosopher David Stove:

> No, Virginia, you and I are not being manipulated by our selfish genes for their own benefit. There are certain people who are subject to incorrigible delusions of being manipulated, and there are also such things as confidence men. But that is all there is to it: there are no "confidence genes." That class of work calls for both intelligence and purpose, and genes have neither. They cannot trick people out of their money by issuing false balance sheets, or writing fraudulent books, or by anything of that kind. (Stove 197)

We are not the victims of 'selfish genes' or parasitizing memes; our minds and souls are our own responsibility (God help us) and cultures are not 'collective fantasies about worlds we cannot see.' Rather, cultures rank among the chief creative works of mankind. "Culture is the concretization—the rendering in some permanent form—of mankind's culturative acts, commonly manifested in man-made objects, structures, texts, etc." (Hegeman 37) Even at his best, a scientist or engineer may contribute to his civilization; but his contribution simply influences that which is greater. The culture is given form by a complex interaction and interconnection of shared language, religion, history, geography, moral standards, political systems and many other factors. Aristotle's wisdom stands to this day: "...every community is established with a view to some good; for mankind always acts in order to obtain that which they think good." (*Politics* I.1) The culture gives expression to the 'highest good' of a people, and each individual within the culture plays a role in its maintenance, affirmation, and even reformation.

Yes, "... every community is established with a view to some good..." I remember when the attendees of the first meeting of the Mars Society met in Boulder back in '98 and all of us had the opportunity to sign the Founding Declaration—not just electronically, but on big broadsheets. Periodically, I like to review that Founding Declaration of the Mars Society,[4] because it reminds me why we are here—it is the statement of the 'good' around which this society is organized. I would encourage you to reread the whole declaration; when you do, you will find that it is not a scientific treatise, nor (thankfully) a series of policy talking points. Instead, it reverberates with cultural themes. Even when scientific matters are referenced, they are not 'abstract'; instead, they are rooted in the needs of humanity: "The time has come for humanity to journey to Mars." This is the 'good' which is at the core of why we are here. It is the civilizational priority: the time has come.

The goals of a civilization set expectations for individuals within the group, but the goals remain beyond the ability of any individual to accomplish. The goal which we share—"The time has come for humanity to journey to Mars"—is not simply a matter of engineering; otherwise, it would have been accomplished. It is for fathers and mothers, school teachers and doctors, engineers and lobbyists, musicians and philosophers, priests and farmers, architects and astronauts—it is for all who share to goal; for all who share the hope for a new world, and participate in their own way in this shared vision. We believe we must go, not because it is easy, not because it is hard, but because we believe it is the right path for humanity at this stage in our history. We might be wrong. We might fail. We might allow ourselves to become distracted, or divided, and waste the opportunity. But the goal remains: "The time has come for humanity to journey to Mars." Consider the following paragraphs from our Founding Declaration:

---

[4] Available online at:
http://www.marssociety.org/portal/groups/tmssc/founding_declaration

We must go for the challenge. Civilizations, like people, thrive on challenge and decay without it. The time is past for human societies to use war as a driving stress for technological progress. As the world moves towards unity, we must join together, not in mutual passivity, but in common enterprise, facing outward to embrace a greater and nobler challenge than that which we previously posed to each other. Pioneering Mars will provide such a challenge. Furthermore, a cooperative international exploration of Mars would serve as an example of how the same joint-action could work on Earth in other ventures.

There are no small number of cultural assumptions within this statement. We do not believe that a civilization is a static thing: there are those civilizations which thrive, and those which decay. There are, we believe, challenges which are noble and thus there are also those which are ignoble. We see the challenge which confronts us as one which might set forth an example for all people—truly, a bold claim.

Frankly, much of the Western world no longer seeks challenges; instead, the majority desire nothing more than personal peace and affluence. Thirty years ago, theologian Francis Schaeffer described the culturally debilitating character of these two ruling desires:

Personal peace means just to be let alone, not to be troubled by the troubles of other people, whether across the world or across the city—to live one's life with minimal possibilities of being personally disturbed. Personal peace means want to have my personal life pattern undisturbed in my lifetime, regardless of what the results will be in the lifetimes of my children and grandchildren. Affluence means an overwhelming and ever-increasing prosperity—a life made up of things and more things—a success judged by an ever-higher level of material abundance. (205)

Of course, such concerns are always with us, but it is a mark of a decaying culture that the majority have focused themselves almost entirely on personal peace and affluence. Civic responsibility—everything from the P.T.A. to service in the Armed Forces, to voting, to acts of charity—is on the decline. Thus Sociologist Douglas Porpora wrote in 2001:

> The problem in the modern or postmodern world is a pervasive loss of emotionally moving contact with a good that is ultimate, a contact that was once provided by the sacred. We are still emotionally moved by goods, but they tend to be goods that are less than ultimate—family, friends, and material possessions. As a consequence, the whole of our lives is without any overarching moral purpose. There is a lot of talk today about our loss of vision, and that is what the loss of overarching moral purpose entails. This hardly means that we are all immoral. It does mean that our sense of morality has become largely procedural. (71–72)

Let's consider another article of the Founding Declaration:

> We must go for the opportunity. The settling of the Martian New World is an opportunity for a noble experiment in which humanity has another chance to shed old baggage and begin the world anew, carrying forward as much of the best of our heritage as possible and leaving the worst behind. Such chances do not come often and are not to be disdained lightly.

Settling a new world is not the end in itself; it serves higher, civilizational and cultural goals. (In Aristotelean terms, one could say that settlement of Mars is a material cause in service of a culturally-determined final cause.) This clause points out that a goal of the Mars Society is the reformation of culture; it is a chance to keep the best of our heritage, and leave behind the worst. There is, perhaps, a touching naivety here, for even the desire for reform still carries with it the taint of that from which one desires to be freed. Our past—as individuals, as a civilization—is always with us, and it remains the context of all our thoughts, words, and actions. Nevertheless, the work is noble and all such efforts to turn from that which is evil and embrace the good is cultural progress, to say the least; one might even call it repentance.

> We must go for our humanity. Human beings are more than merely another kind of animal—we are life's messenger. Alone of the creatures of the Earth, we have the ability to continue the work of creation by bringing life to Mars, and Mars to life. In doing so, we shall make a profound statement as to the precious worth of the human race and every member of it.

This is, for me, perhaps the most fascinating statement in the entire declaration. In the dreadful ideology of the 'Terrible Simplifiers,' humanity is reduced to just another kind of animal, and all life to a freak accident of chemistry; indeed, life is somewhat of an embarrassing accident of chemistry, since it has given rise to all kinds of questions which make modern man uncomfortable. In the face such antihuman ideology, we affirm that we are part of "creation," and in fact the only creatures of Earth with the ability to "continue the work of creation..." The human race ("...and every member of it") is of "precious worth." We have witnessed the century of greatest slaughter in human history. There are those who wickedly engage in statistical games which seek to obscure this fact, but the reality remains, and we can feel it to the core of our beings. Many who claimed to have sought to slay God and have simply slain humanity by the millions—the 'mere statistics' of Stalin. In opening a new world, it is right that we should affirm that every human life is precious—we are not a mistake, or an accident, either as a species or as individuals. In the wake of so much death and suffering, there is a desperate need to affirm the value of life.

"What is a new civilization worth?" This is a question which feels much like asking the value of human life itself. It is not a question of engineering or chemistry or physics; no, it is of a higher order than those fields are equipped to answer. As a result, in a technophilic age such as ours, there is a danger that the question will be avoided. Fortunately, it is one which is addressed in the popular culture through the means of fiction. Almost all of the enduring works of science fiction have been about civilization and culture, not about technology; the 'hard science fiction' works tend to have a pretty short 'shelf life' for the cutting edge science of the moment is absurdly wrong before long. No, humanity's stories are about people, and that is the way it should be.

Today, I would like for you to briefly consider a short story that was written over 50 years ago, "Crucifixus Etiam," by Walter M. Miller, Jr. Miller is best remembered today for his novel, *A Canticle for Leibowitz* (1959), and Miller publish his "Crucifixus Etiam" six years earlier. The story is set in the year 2134, and the main character in the story is Manue Nanti, a young man from Peru who has been lured to Mars by the promise of quickly getting rich. He has come to serve out a five year contract, and his hope is simply that at the end of his five years he could return to Earth and retire at the age of twenty-four. "Manue wanted to travel, to see the far corners of the world, the strange cultures, the simple people, the small towns, deserts, mountains, jungles—for until he came to Mars, he had never been farther than a hundred miles from Cerro de Pasco, his birthplace in Peru." (100) Manue wanted personal peace and affluence; he wanted the financial liberty to pursue his personal interests, and Mars was nothing to him but a means to accomplish that end.

But there was a problem; as Miller wrote it (according to the science of the time) each worker underwent a surgery in a which a 'mechanical oxygenator' was grafted into the body to pull what little oxygen was available from the thin Martian air; breathing was unnecessary, except to provide wind for talking. And most Martian workers soon gave in, and allowed their lungs to atrophy, making it virtually impossible to live a normal life again.

The story centers in Manue's dilemma: he went to Mars to 'get rich quick'; but he quickly realized that the Red Planet would almost certainly deprive him of the joy of life, and would take from him something which almost any young person takes for granted: the ability simply to breathe. At nineteen, Manue learned a lesson that most people run away from their whole life: what is the point of living for personal peace and affluence, which quickly are lost in death? Manue did not even have the satisfaction of being a 'zealot' for the work; the Mars Project was employment, not a labor of love.

Miller explains,

The Mars Project had started eighty or ninety years ago, and its end goal was to make Mars habitable for colonists without Earth support, without oxies and insulated suits and the various gadgets a man now had to use to keep himself alive on the fourth planet. But thus far,

Earth had planted without reaping. The sky was a bottomless well into which Earth poured her tools, dollars, manpower, and engineering skill. And there appeared to be no hope for the near future. (109)

The workers themselves are extremely cynical about the project; as a co-worker tells Manue:

So, it's either cut production or find an outlet. Mars is an outlet for surplus energies, manpower, money. Mars Project keeps money turning over, keeps everything turning over. Economist told me that. Said if the Project folded, surplus would pile up—big depression on Earth.

The Peruvian shook his head and sighed. It didn't sound right somehow. It sounded like an explanation somebody figured out after the whole thing started. It wasn't the kind of goal he wanted. (114–115)

Personal prosperity isn't enough; even global prosperity isn't enough to give purpose to life and death.

But the project wasn't just another contractor's 'sinkhole.' In fact, the hole which Manue and the other workers were digging was one of three hundred wells, boring deep into the Martian soil, to reach clathrates buried deep underground; Kinley, an engineer, explains that "Three hundred wells, working for eight centuries, can get the job done." (122) As atmosphere begins to pour from the well he had helped to dig, Manue realized he could breathe it in:

But lungs were clogged, and he could not drink of the racing wind. His big calloused hand clutched slowly at the ground, and he choked a brief sound like a sob.

A shadow fell over him. It was Kinley, come to offer his thanks for the quelling of Handell. But he said

17

nothing for a moment as he watched Manue's desperate Gethsemane.

"Some sow, others reap," he said.

"Why?" the Peruvian choked.

The supervisor shrugged. "What's the difference? But if you can't be both, which would you rather be?"

Nanti looked up into the wind. He imagined a city to the south, a city built on tear-soaked ground, filled with people who had no ends beyond their culture, no goal but within their own society. It was a good sensible question: Which would he rather be—a sower or reaper?

...

He knew now what Mars was—not a ten-thousand-a-year job, not a garbage can for surplus production. But an eight-century passion of human faith in the destiny of the race of Man. He paused short of the truck. He had wanted to travel, to see the sights of Earth, the handiwork of Nature and of history, the glorious places of his planet.

He stooped, and scooped up a handful of the red-brown soil, letting it sift slowly between his fingers. Here was Mars—his planet now. No more of Earth, not for Manue Nanti. He adjusted his aerator more comfortably and climbed into the waiting truck. (126-7)

Manue Nanti was seized by an ethic of self-sacrifice; a man who first saw Mars as a means to selfish fulfillment, but found purpose which surpassed him, and allowed him to offer himself as a sacrifice for the destiny of the race of Man. The title of the story, "Crucifixus Etiam," comes from the first two Latin

18

words for the clause of the Creed, "He was crucified also for us under Pontius Pilate".

Do you want to be a sower or a reaper? You cannot reap of Mars; if you desire to reap, then your rewards are here and now, in your own peace and affluence. But if you desire to help build a world, and to affirm with your life all that there may be part of the destiny of the race of Man upon the sands of Mars, stand with us. There is great value in beginning to learn again how to live for more than yourself; and perhaps in learning to so live, you may find your own sacrifice is at it's best, but a pale reflection of a far greater sacrifice which has already been made for you.

Cited Works:

Hegeman, Bruce David, *Plowing in Hope—Toward a Biblical Theology of Culture* (Moscow, Idaho: Canon Press, 2004)

Kirk, Russell, "Can We Apprehend Science?," in *The Intemperate Professor and other Cultural Splenetics* (Peru, Illinois: Sherwood Sugden & Co., 1988)

Miller, Walter M., Jr., "Crucifixus Etiam," in *Tomorrow's Worlds* (New York: Meredith Press, 1969)

Porpora, Douglas, *Landscapes of the Soul, the Loss of Moral Meaning in American Life* (Oxford: Oxford University Press, 2001)

Schaeffer, Francis, *How Should We Then Live?*, (Wheaton, Illinois: Crossway Books, 1976)

Wilkins, John, *The Discovery of a World in the Moone, or, a Discourse tending to Prove, that 'tis probable there may be another habitable World in that Planet*, (London: Michael Sparl and Edward Forrest, 1638). Reprinted in facsimile in 1972 by Theatrum Orbis Terrarum Ltd., Amsterdam.

II. Virtue and the Settlement of a New World[5]

Abstract:

Discussions of space exploration rarely mention such 'abstractions' as virtue; such a concept is almost seen as a weakness in contrast to bold plans to open a new world. This presentation takes issue with such dismissive assessments, because the settlement of a new world is more than engineering. In fact, apart from pursuit of virtue, such efforts are certainly failure. A study of ethical implications of proposed courses of action should help guide discussions of settling a new world. This presentation will explore elements of the rounded human character needed on the Martian frontier, and the relationship of the four cardinal virtues (fortitude, justice, temperance and prudence) will be defined and related to character in such a settlement.

*****

On October 4, 2007, the world briefly noted the fiftieth anniversary of space flight which began with the launch of Sputnik 1, but the dream of space flight is far older than the Cold War, and the link between space exploration and new frontiers goes back much further. The Lutheran theologian and astronomer Johannes Kepler wrote his *Somnium* circulated his in 1611 wherein he imagined viewing Earth from the vantage point of the moon. In 1638, Vicar John Wilkins speculated about the prospects of men setting forth into space after the fashion of the great explorers of the terrestrial globe:

In the first ages of the world the Islanders either thought themselves to be the only dwellers upon the earth, or else if there were any other, yet they could not possibly conceive how they might have any commerce with them, being severed by the deep and broad Sea, but the after-times found out the invention of ships, in which notwithstanding none but some bold daring men durst

---

[5] This essay was first presented to the tenth annual international convention of the Mars Society, meeting at U.C.L.A., August 30–September 2, 2007.

venture, there being few so resolute as to commit themselves unto the vast Ocean, and yet now how easy a
thing is this, even to a timorous and cowardly nature?
So, perhaps, there may be some other means invented
for a conveyance to the Moon, and though it may seem
a terrible and impossible thing ever to pass through the
vast spaces of the air, yet no question there would be
some men who durst venture this as well as the other.
True indeed, I cannot conceive any possible means for
the like discovery of this conjecture, since there can be
no sailing to the Moon, unless that were true which the
Poets do but feign, that she made her bed in the Sea. We
have not now any *Drake* or *Columbus* to undertake this voyage, or any *Daedalus* to invent a conveyance through
the air. However, I doubt not but that time which is still
the father of new truths, and hath revealed unto us
many things which our Ancestors were ignorant of, will
also manifest to our posterity, that which we now desire, but cannot know. (*A World in the Moon* 207–9)

Wilkins was no idle speculator, for he would later serve as a
bishop in the Church of England until his death in 1672, and
also distinguished himself as a founder, and first secretary, of
the Royal Society.

Wilkins recognized that an endeavor such as space
flight would require a spirit of boldness, typified (in his words)
in the persons of Francis Drake and Christopher Columbus,
combined with the technological prowess of the mythical
Daedalus. In Wilkins' bold words, it was a matter of waiting
for such to be "manifest to our posterity." Three and a quarter
centuries later, we are, by and large, still waiting. The skill of a
Daedalus was manifest already nearly forty years ago. But the
virtue which Wilkins identified in the great explorers has not

been manifest in sufficient quantity for a *capacity* for exploration to become manifest in *action*. When we speak of a frontier, we are speaking in terms of settlement and for at least the past two to three generations, the beginning of settlement has been envisioned as 'at least a generation or two in the future,' and shows no sign of drawing nearer in the foreseeable future.

Back in 1983, Los Alamos hosted a Conference on Interstellar Migration, the proceedings of which were published in *Interstellar Migration and the Human Experience*. One of the presenters was Douglas Schwartz, who was then President of the School of American Research in Santa Fe. Schwartz addressed the topic, "The Colonizing Experience: A Cross-Cultural Perspective." His analysis of thirteen postmigration communities is particularly interesting because it was not limited to the experiences of a narrow range of human experience, but was quite diverse in terms of culture, history, level of technology, and environmental challenges. In concluding his analysis, Schwartz identified "five groups of critical variables relating to migration": motivation, environment, structure, process, and culture. Weighing all these factors, Schwartz observed,

> Finally, while all these variables are at work, the most important factor is still the nature of the basic culture. The value system and its strength, the migrants' orientation toward change and individuality, how malcontents are to be dealt with, and a host of similar abstract issues may have more effect on the resulting success of the new settlement than all the other determinants combined.

> The two most important variables emerging from this review that can be controlled to some extent before a migration and that bear on its ultimate outcome are the interrelated factors of group cohesiveness and degree of individualism. It would appear that, all other

things being equal, a successful migration depends upon a strong group orientation. (245)

Schwartz's observation, then, is that the issue of opening a new frontier is not, primarily, one of technology, but of culture. (In fact, technology really only entered into his discussion in terms of the effect on a future culture which environmental challenges would force on settlement populations.) Thus, the solution is not to be found in the workshop of Daedalus.

The presenter realizes that this is not likely to be a popular opinion in some circles, but it certainly speaks to the relative lack of progress toward the new frontier which stands in stark contrast to the tremendous technological advances which have occurred during the past half century. Neither the societal elites, nor the broader masses of public opinion, feel or express a manifest need to pursue opening a new frontier. An appetite for science fiction does not translate to a pursuit of science fact.

Perhaps some would counter that the thoughts of the average "man in the street" were no more elevated in other ages and cultures which witnessed the opening of great frontiers. Of course, that view is nothing other than a projection of current cultural expectations on other periods and cultures of human experience. But it is also precisely misses the point. The culture sets forth the expectation for the conduct of individuals within the group; the individual evaluates himself, and is evaluated by others, in terms of his adherence to those cultural expectations. To speak plainly, it is far from necessary for a civilization to be made up of individuals such as Francis Drake or Christopher Columbus (to continue Wilkins' point of comparison); but it does make a huge difference whether such individuals are perceived as standard bearers of a cultural norm or ideal. What is at issue, then, is whether our culture is one which idealizes individual risk for the sake of the community, and particularly individual risk for the sake of establishing a community on a new frontier. For all of their faults, the cultures which opened the last frontier did manifest such an idealization—men were afforded acclaim, renown, title, wealth and other societal rewards because of the risks which they assumed for the sake of community.

Such risks and rewards are not that far removed from our culture, historically speaking. The last great flowering of such sentiments were probably manifested in those men and women who explored and settled the Soviet and Canadian Arctic. However, I do not include early participants in the American and Soviet space programs in this category because their fame was and is not associated with opening new areas to human settlement, per se, but for having explored an almost unimaginably hostile environment and returned to tell the tale. Perhaps it could be said that we do not lack for 'Magellans,'[6] but as yet we have not had our Columbus or Drake.

The dilemma which confronts us, and which presently delays human expansion into the solar system is not something as easily solved as technological development. The problem is cultural, and this problem is far more difficult to address. Cultural problems do not have a ready solution; there is not some "plug and play" upgrade which will come out in another eighteen months in Beta release.

Therefore, the presenter chooses to address this issue in terms of virtue. This term is, perhaps, somewhat problematic because the present deterioration of our language has debased the term in the usage of much of the English-speaking world to an airy discussion of morality. That is not the concern under consideration in this presentation. Rather, we are using the term

---

[6] Although we might still marvel at a generation willing to send 270 men on a mission from which only 18 would return.

virtue according to the Greek and Latin words from which the concept is derived, *ethike arete* (or "habitual excellence") and *virtus* ("the power to accomplish"). In this proper sense, the virtues are those habitual powers which are capable of accomplishing that which is good.

Traditionally, the West has spoken of the four "cardinal" virtues of temperance, prudence, fortitude, and justice.[7] The problematic matter of defining these terms is made worse by the misuse of several of these terms in modern English. The following definitions will suffice for purposes of this presentation: "temperance" refers to moderation and restraint; "prudence" is the wisdom to render ethical judgments; "fortitude" comprehends both physical and moral courage, and thus the ability to withstand danger, fear, pain, intimidation, or the temptation to despair; "justice" is that virtue by which that which is right is rendered to the individual and to the community.

Since at least the third century B.C., there has been a fundamental divide within Western civilization between competing systems which may broadly be referred to as Epicureanism[8] (or Utilitarianism) and Stoicism[9]. In generalized terms, Epicureanism maintains that the "good," or virtuous, is that which brings the greatest happiness, while Stoicism maintains that one should be indifferent to pain or pleasure, in pursuit of a moral standard outside of, and superior to, man. For the

---

[7] Additionally, there are also the three "theological" virtues of faith, hope and love (or charity).

[8] named for Epicurus of Samos (341–270 B.C.), and best known in the Latin West through the writings of Lucretius, a contemporary of the Stoic Cicero.

[9] founded by Zeno of Citium (335–263 B.C.), and best exemplified in the Latin West through the writings of Cicero (106–43 B.C.) and Seneca (4 B.C.–65 A.D.). The Stoics take their name of the *Stoa Poecile* ("Painted Porch") in Athens where Zeno lectured.

Stoic, the pursuit of truth is a fundamental characteristic of man; in the words of Cicero, "Above all, the search after truth and its eager pursuit are peculiar to man. And so, when we have leisure from the demands of business care, we are eager to see, to hear, to learn something new, and we esteem a desire to know the secrets or wonders of creation as indispensable to a happy life." (*De Officiis* 15)

Epicurean thought purports to be concerned with virtue, even in the conventional sense of the term, but it is does not share the Stoic's concern for truth, or the needs of the community. For the Epicurean, personal pleasure and the avoidance of pain form the sole standard of life; thus, the motivation for avoiding injustice is fear of punishment, not the pursuit of virtue and truth for their own sake. The most that the Epicurean will concede is "The just life is most free from disturbance, but the unjust life is full of the greatest disturbance." (*Principle Doctrines* 33) Again, "Injustice is not a bad thing in its own right, but [only] because of the fear produced by the suspicion that one will not escape the notice of those assigned to punish such actions." (35) Such a statement of ambivalence to justice and injustice is the height of depravity to a Stoic. Since for the Epicurean the sole standard of action, or inaction, is not transcendent, but immanent (that is, existing only in the mind of the individual), there is no necessity of service or justice to others, or to future generations. In fact, self-sacrifice for the benefit of those unborn would be a violation of the Epicurean ethic: "He who has learned the limits of life knows that it is easy to provide that which removes the feeling of pain owing to want and one's whole life perfect. So there is no need for things which involve struggle." (34) Epicureanism is a doctrine of stagnation.

Stoicism, with its emphasis on duty to transcendent virtue, is oriented toward that which is above man—the pursuit of truth, and thus the pursuit of virtue, despite any personal sacrifice or struggle. In the words of Cicero,

> The soul that is altogether courageous and great is marked above all by two characteristics: one of these is indifference to outward circumstances; for such a person cherishes the conviction that nothing but moral goodness and propriety deserves to be either admired or wished for or striven after, and that he ought not to be subject to any man or any passion or any accident of fortune. The second characteristic is that, when the soul is disciplined in the way above mentioned, one should do deeds not only great and in the highest degree useful, but extremely arduous and laborious and fraught with danger both to life and to many things that make life worth living. (*De Officiis* 69)

However, Epicureanism is fundamentally sensate, maintaining that there is nothing above that which is accessible to the senses, and the virtue of a thing is found in its appeal to the senses. The result is a world view which is primarily turned inward on the individual and his perception of his desires. The highest aim of the Epicurean is not the pursuit of truth, but of pleasure. All morality is relativized, so that it is taught, "Justice was not a thing in its own right, but [exists] in mutual dealings in whatever places there [is] a pact about neither harming one another nor being harmed." (*Principle Doctrines* 35)

The Epicurean world view is always asking, in essence, "What's in it for me?" And thus he would evaluate virtue itself. Seneca offers the Epicurean a harsh retort, "Therefore you blunder when you ask what it is that makes me seek virtue; you are looking for something beyond the supreme. Do you ask what it is that I seek in virtue? Only herself. For she offers nothing better—she herself is her own reward." (*De Vita Beata* 123) Again, Seneca asks,

> And how shall Virtue guide Pleasure if she follows her, since it is the part of one who obeys to follow, or one who commands to guide? ... Let virtue go first, let her bear the standard. We shall none the less have pleasure, but we shall be the master and control her; at times we shall yield to her entreaty, never to her constraint. But those who surrender the leadership to pleasure, lack both; for they lose virtue, and yet do not possess pleasure, but are possessed by it, and they are either tortured by the lack of it or strangled by its excess—wretched if it deserts them, more wretched if it overwhelms them... (123)

As Anne Glyn-Jones noted in *Holding up a Mirror—How Civilizations Decline*, "It is no coincidence that the centuries during which Lucretius's Epicureanism was a dominant influence on Roman thought encompassed the most materially prosperous years of the whole Roman epoch." (120) Seneca, reflecting on the Epicureanism which followed in the wake of Lucretius, declared, "And so it is not Epicurus who has driven them to debauchery, but they, having surrendered themselves to vice, hide their debauchery in the lap of philosophy and flock to the place where they may hear the praise of pleasure". (129) Thus it is understood that Epicureanism is ever the philosophical 'fig leaf' sought as a cover for abandoning any responsibility to society, family, or culture for the sake of indulging the self.

As noted before, the Stoics were outward in their orientation, with virtue and the pursuit of truth as the measure of a life well-lived. As Cicero observed that the pursuit of truth was the peculiar pursuit of man, and the greatest happiness of man, so Seneca observed the same virtue, and declared that this character led to the study of the heavens:

> Nature has bestowed upon us an inquisitive disposition, and being well aware of her own skill and beauty, has begotten us as spectators of her mighty array, since she would lose the fruit of her labour if her works, so vast, so glorious, so artfully contrived, so bright and so beautiful in more ways than one, were displayed to a lonely solitude. That you may understand how she wished us, not merely to behold her, but to gaze upon her, see the position in which she has placed us. She has set us in the center of her creation, and has granted us a view that sweeps the universe; and she has not only created man erect, but in order to fit him for contemplation of herself, she has given him a head to top the body, and set it upon a pliant neck, in order that he might follow the stars as they glide from their rising to their setting and turn his face about with the whole revolving heaven. And besides, guiding on their course six constellations by day, and six by night, she left no part of herself unrevealed, hoping that by these wonders which she had presented to man's eyes she might also arouse his curiosity in the rest. For we have not beheld them all, nor the full compass of them, but our vision opens up a path for its investigation, and lays the foundations of truth so that our research may pass from revealed to hidden things and discover something more ancient than the world itself—whence yon stars came forth, what was the state of the universe before the several elements separated to form its parts, what principle separated the engulfed and confused elements, who appointed their places to things, whether the heavy elements sank and the light ones flew aloft by reason of

their own nature, or apart from the energy and gravity of matter some higher power has appointed laws for each of them... Our thought burst through the ramparts of the sky, and is not content to know that which is revealed. (*De Otio* 191-193)

Seneca's complaint against the Epicureans was that they would not turn their eyes "from human affairs to the things of heaven." (*De Otio* 195) And this is one of the problems with Epicureanism in our own age, as well. Engaging personal risk for the sake of virtue and the pursuit of truth is unthinkable for the Epicurean, and it is a necessity for the Stoic. The conclusion of Seneca's *De Otio* speaks directly to our topic at hand: "If anyone says that the best life of all is to sail the sea, and then adds that I must not sail upon a sea where shipwrecks are a common occurrence and there are often sudden storms that sweep the helmsman in an adverse direction, I conclude that this man, although he lauds navigation, really forbids me to launch my ship." (201)

The Epicurean will never leave harbor; in fact, the Epicurean will never build ships in the first place, unless his pleasure is assured, and his safety secured. Epicureanism flourished in the midst of the wealth of Rome, and lacking the character of self-sacrifice which established the *Pax Romana*, Rome fell into decline. Epicureans will spend billions to secure their luxuries, but will never reach beyond this world, for they will always perceive a safer profit at home; sacrifice of one's own wealth, comfort, even life, for the sake of future generations is madness to the Epicurean, whereas it is the highest virtue to the Stoic. Prudence, Fortitude, Justice, and Temperance—though despised by the Epicurean—are necessary for the opening of a new frontier. Without the willingness to sacrifice comfort for the sake of virtue, truth will be despised.

Consider, in brief, some of the implications for the four cardinal virtues—prudence, fortitude, justice and temperance—in the context of establishing and sustaining civilization. It is also important to understand the meaning of the terms, so that we may comprehend the character of the Virtue.

Prudence (or **Wisdom**) ranks as chief among the cardinal virtues, and to a certain extent the other Virtues depend upon Prudence. Thus Cicero observes,

> Now, of the four divisions which we have made of the essential idea of moral goodness, the first, consisting in the knowledge of truth, touches human nature most closely. For we are all attracted and drawn to a zeal for learning and knowing; and we think it glorious to excel therein, while we count it base and immoral to fall into error, to wander from the truth, to be ignorant, to be led astray. In this pursuit, which is both natural and morally right, two errors are to be avoided: first, we must not treat the unknown as known and too readily accept it; and he who wishes to avoid this error (as all should do) will devote both time and attention to the weighing of evidence. The other error is that some people devote too much industry and too deep study to matters that are obscure and difficult and useless as well." (*De Officiis* 19–21)

Or as we read in the Proverbs of Solomon:

> Happy is the man who finds wisdom, and the man who gains understanding; for her proceeds are better than the profits of silver, and her gain than fine gold. She is more precious than rubies, and all the things you may desire cannot compare with her. Length of days is in her right hand, in her left hand richest and honor. Her ways are ways of pleasantness, and all her paths are peace. She is a tree of life to those who take hold of her, and

happy are all who retain her. ... My son, let them not depart from your eyes—keep sound wisdom and discretion; so they will be life to your soul and grace to your neck. Then you will walk safely in your way, and your foot will not stumble. (3:13–18; 21–23 NKJV)

Wisdom discerns the motivation for action, or inaction, and weighs such motivations in the balance, rendering a judgment in keeping with the Virtues.

Fortitude is also known as **Courage**. Fortitude, when combined with Wisdom, confronts fear, danger, even death, with the will to act, or refrain from action, to the benefit of Society. People are accustomed in our age to think primarily in terms of physical courage, but it is by no means limited in that fashion. Again, Cicero defined the courageous soul as being "marked above all by two characteristics: one of these is indifference to outward circumstances; for such a person cherishes the conviction that nothing but moral goodness and propriety deserves to be either admired or wished for or striven after ... The second characteristic is that ... one should do deeds not only great and in the highest degree useful, but extremely arduous and laborious and fraught with danger both to life and to many things that make life worth living." (69) Epicureans have no place in their system for courage—but such an indifference to personal circumstance is what is needed on the frontier.

Justice is coupled with Wisdom and Courage; thus Cicero: "And so we demand that men who are courageous and high-souled shall at the same time be good and straightforward, lovers of truth, and foes of deception; for these qualities are the centre and soul of justice." (69) In light of Schwartz's observations that "a successful migration depends upon a strong group orientation" in the importance of justice is crucial; members of a community must have the assurance of relatively just treatment by their fellow members of society, and must be concerned personally with upholding justice toward their fellow citizens.

Temperance concerns the limitation of appetites according to the bounds of reason. Cicero placed it in relation to the other Virtues: "Now we find that the essential activity of the spirit is twofold: one force is appetite (that is *orme*, in Greek), which impels a man this way and that; the other is reason, which teaches and explains what should be done and what should be left undone. The result is that reason commands, appetite obeys." (103) Presently, men are often viewed at little more than beasts, incapable of self-restraint. When human beings allow themselves to be defined as "consumers," there is little desire among cultural elites to encourage temperance; rather, the more intemperate the better, so that even more production may be consumed. Healthy civilizations require temperance—duty must come before individual whims and appetites.

A civilization centered on the cultivation of the virtues, with the attendant pursuit of truth, and self-sacrifice for the sake of that which is good, is a culture which expands and flourishes, while the Epicurean pursuit of personal happiness, lends to decline and decadence—these are facts to which human experience gives ample testimony. But the pursuit of Virtue does not collapse into simply being "Anti-Epicurean"—one does not pursue Virtue to avoid the decline attendant to the triumph of Epicurus; one cultivates Virtue irrespective of personal cost, and one result of such willingness for self-sacrifice is the benefit which it provides to the entire society.

At present, citizens are willing to be described as "consumers"; they do not defend their identity in the context of relationship to Church, State, and Family—the traditional "Three Estates"—but are content it would seem, to have their existence defined by their capacity to consume goods and services—an astonishing surrender for a free people, and which abandons virtue for the pursuit of the truth.

Much has been said and written about the tremendous technological advances which the current generations have witnessed. Undoubtedly, the public will support billions and trillions of dollars being invested in technologies which are perceived to be of immediate benefit to themselves: medical technologies and consumer electronics continue to rise in demand. With estimates now placing Apple's iPod sales in the neighborhood of 12 million a quarter by next year[10] one can readily see that it is not that Western civilization has suddenly become Luddite. But unless your goal is to watch "Mission to Mars" on a iPod on your flight home from this conference, one would be hard pressed to demonstrate the broad based cultural support for developing the technologies for a *real* mission to Mars.

With a FY 2007 NASA budget of $16.1 billion, one can hardly imagine how quickly we could get to Mars if Americans were willing to devote as much money a year to that program as they invest in consumer electronics. It is at this point that most efforts to 'convince' the public of the merits of space exploration have fallen short: the dominant view within Western civilization is materialistic, self-centered—in short, Epicurean. Because of this mindset, such people will not support such a program of exploration unless they perceive it to be of immediate benefit to them. Promises of benefits—or threats—to future generations means very little to people who have decided not to have children because it "cramps their lifestyle."

In his 1947 book, *The Abolition of Man,* C. S. Lewis identified the nature of our dilemma:

---

[10] http://www.appleinsider.com/articles/07/05/08/
caris_sees_iphone_sales_topping_25_million_per_year_by_09.html

And all the time—such is the tragi-comedy of our situation—we continue to clamour for those very qualities we are rendering impossible. You can hardly open a periodical without coming across the statement that what our civilization needs is more 'drive,' or dynamism, or self-sacrifice, or 'creativity.' In a sort of ghastly simplicity we remove the organ and demand the function. We make men without chests and expect of them virtue and enterprise. We laugh at honor and are shocked to find traitors in our midst. We castrate and bid the geldings be fruitful. (35)

The predominant technological pursuits of the West are Epicurean in orientation. We do not lack for a Daedalus; his workshops are rather busy, actually, in the endless pursuit of conveniences, comforts, and indulgences in service of a desiccated materialism promulgated by the "hollow men," of whom T. S. Eliot wrote so eloquently. We have been here before: we have come full circle to the rationalization-as-philosophy of the Ancient Epicureans. It is a civilizational dead end.

We lack a Columbus or a Drake, and we shall not see them, until we lift our eyes to the pursuit of virtue. In this task, there is no "quick fix," only personal commitment. When our culture has done that, perhaps it may begin once again to seek the Font of the love of virtue, and the zeal for truth. Again, we have been here before. The solution may again be found in the application of the insights of Aristotle's *Nicomachean Ethics*, once read through the lense of St. Thomas Aquinas' observations, in the cultivation of the *habitus* of virtue. Thus manifested in action, the virtues so tragically neglected in our modern age could find expression in the settlement of a New World. In the repudiation of Epicureanism, and the pursuit and cultivation of virtue, we submit to the reality that there is a significance to human life and action which exceeds our present understanding and estimation. This brings us to the theological virtues —faith, hope, and love— and a topic for another occasion.

Works Cited:

Cicero, *De Officiis*, trans. by Walter Miller (Cambridge, Massachusetts: Harvard University Press, 2005)

Epicurus, *The Principal Doctrines* XIV in *The Epicurus Reader*, trans. and ed. by Brad Inwood and L.P. Gerson (Indianapolis: Hackett Publishing Company, 1994)

Glyn-Jones, Anne, *Holding up a Mirror—How Civilizations Decline*

Lewis, C.S., *The Abolition of Man*, (New York: HarperCollins, 1947)

Schwarz, Douglas, "The Colonizing Experience: A Cross-Cultural Perspective" in *Interstellar Migration and the Human Experience,* edited by Ben R. Finney and Eric M. Jones (University of California Press: Berkeley, 1985)

Seneca, *De Otio* and *De Vita Beata* in *Moral Essays Volume II* (Cambridge, Massachusetts: Harvard University Press, 2001)

Wilkins, John, *The Discovery of a World in the Moone, or, a Discourse tending to Prove, that 'tis probable there may be another habitable World in that Planet*, (London: Michael Sparl and Edward Forrest, 1638). Reprinted in facsimile in 1972 by Theatrum Orbis Terrarum Ltd., Amsterdam.

III. "Space Exploration and Christian Hope— Charting a Course between Utopia and Dystopia."[11]

Abstract:

Building on last year's consideration of the role of the cardinal virtues (fortitude, justice, temperance and prudence) as motivations for space exploration and settlement, this presentation will explore the relationship between the virtue of hope and the motivation for human expansion into the solar system, beginning with Mars. Space exploration and settlement are often cast either in terms of a new paradise or utter disaster— either utopia or dystopia. Such extremes are a Scylla and Charybdis for such efforts, raising impossible expectations on the one hand, and irrational fears on the other. Human exploration and settlement is a story of community, and where there is community, there is the opportunity for the exercise of the virtues as a necessary component of a thriving civilization.

*****

It was ten years ago—almost to the day—that the Mars Society adopted its Founding Declaration while meeting here at the University of Colorado. That declaration is not lengthy, but it is bold in enumerating the reasons why humanity must journey to Mars. At the heart of the declaration is the assertion that "We must go for the challenge," and it elaborates on that challenge as follows: "Civilizations, like people, thrive on challenge and decay without it. The time is past for human societies to use war as a driving stress for technological progress. As the world moves toward unity, we must join together, not in mutual passivity, but in common enterprise, facing outward to embrace a greater and nobler challenge than that which we previously posed to each other." Again, the declaration asserted that "We must go for the opportunity," because "The settling of the Mar-

---

[11] This essay was first presented to the eleventh annual international convention of the Mars Society, meeting at U.C.—Boulder in August 2008.

tian New World is an opportunity for a noble experiment in which humanity has another chance to shed old baggage and begin the world anew; carrying forward as much of the best of our heritage as possible and leaving the worst behind. Such chances do not come often, and are not to be disdained lightly."

Declaring the exploration of a new world to be a "nobler challenge" and a "noble experiment" is to proclaim that it shows high moral qualities, or a greatness of character. To speak of the nobility of a course of action is to speak of it in terms of the pursuit of Virtue.

Last year, while exploring the theme, "Virtue and the Settlement of a New World," the presenter analyzed our current civilization in terms of the ancient categories of Stoic and Epicurean philosophical systems, and observed that "A civilization centered on the cultivation of the virtues, with the attendant pursuit of truth and self-sacrifice for the sake of that which is good, is a culture which expands and flourishes, while the Epicurean pursuit of personal happiness, lends to decline and decadence— these are facts to which human experience gives amply testimony." As was observed on that occasion, one does not pursue Virtue for the sake of avoiding the decline which is attendant with the rise of Epicureanism; one "cultivates Virtue irrespective of personal cost, and one result of such willingness for self-sacrifice is the benefit which it provides to the entire society." It is precisely in the service of such a cultivation of Virtue that the work of the Mars Society was begun.

Last year, the discussion of the importance of the cultivation of the Virtues to the establishment of civilization on a new world centered on the four cardinal virtues of fortitude, justice, temperance and prudence. On this occasion, and in keeping with the theme of this track, "Space and Religion," it is our intention to address one of the theological virtues—hope—in this essay. In his first epistle, St. Peter exhorts the Church, "But sanctify the Lord God in your hearts, and always *be* ready to *give* a defense to everyone who asks you a reason for the hope that is in you, with meekness and fear" (1 Pet. 3:15 NKJV). Ours is an age in which such hope needs an *apologia*—a defense—and that is our purpose here today.

As fortitude, justice, temperance and prudence are bound together as the cardinal virtues, so the theological virtues of faith, hope, and love are joined together, as well; in the words of St. Paul, "And now abide faith, hope, love, these three; but the greatest of these *is* love." (1 Cor. 13:13) As with the cardinal virtues, the theological virtues are not abstracted from human behavior, but define human existence in conformity with the purpose for its creation. Each of the theological virtues confronts a corresponding vice— vices which are the absence of the virtue. Thus love overcomes hatred, faith overcomes unbelief, hope overcomes despair.

Despair is, arguably, the chief vice of our age, for it rests near the root of the assault on all Virtue—the assault on the very *notion* of Virtue—and despair is part of the appeal of Epicurean phantasms in the minds of men. Despair has come to reign in the hearts and minds of many who now see no purpose to their lives beyond the acquisition of material luxuries. Thus men and women allow themselves to be called "consumers". Now the creation of an appetite for goods is more important than the creation of the goods themselves; in the words of historian John Lukacs: "It may be said that the production of consumption has become more important than the production of goods. While in the past a respected industrialist was someone who was successful in creating production, now he is someone who creates consumption." (Lukacs 19) Consumerism—what was once, more honestly, referred to as gluttony—has no place for hope in any meaningful sense of the virtue, for it does not acknowledge any claim of the past or the future on the present.

It is a failed culture which lives by the credo expressed by Saul Bloom in *Ocean's Twelve*: "I want the last check I write to bounce."

But if we are no longer willing to see ourselves bound by obligations to those who have come before us and to generations yet unborn, having become uprooted from our place in this created order, we no longer know who we are. As sociologist Douglas Porpora recently wrote: "If to know who we are is to know our place in the cosmos, then we cannot lose our place in the cosmos without losing ourselves as well." (Porpora 152)

The false hopes extended by Utopianism in all of its various forms appeals to those who have become uprooted in this fashion, because Utopianism promises a paradise (terrestrial, or extraterrestrial) which is not *beyond* time, but *in* time; a paradise in which one generation never faces the day when it must hand all things on to the next generation.

Despair and Utopianism are thus joined together like two hands of the same body laboring together toward the same end. Since the time of the Renaissance, the ideology of "Progress", under many guises and schemes of men, has promised a Utopia, and each time Progress has proven to be an idol, and its prophets false, and each time devastation and despair have been left in the wake of such movement. Often the Utopians—even when speaking in the dull grey tones of Marxism or shrill, hysterical tones of the Nazis—have borrowed the language of mystics such as Joachim of Fiore (1135–1202) or Tommaso Campanella (1568-1639), as each new movement has promised the imminent arrival of a new Age of Man or "City of the Sun" which will end the 'infancy' or 'adolescence' of man, followed by maturity and endless freedom. Each time, the prophets of Progress have held up the image of a Utopia which is just out of reach— and which nevertheless, will "soon" be attained, when the self-designated elite is allowed to reshape the world in their own image. As perfection is impossible in this world, and Utopia is, literally, "no-place," those who have followed the siren song of Utopianism have gone down to shipwreck, leaving death and despair in the wake of each movement.

The realm of science fiction finds a key element of its commentary on modern society in the guise of exploring possible futures. The result is often insightful analysis—not only of mundane matters such as trends of technological development, but even into the things that truly matter, such as insights into the spirit of the age. But it also yields many attempts to portray a future for man among the stars cast either in terms of a paradise or disaster—Utopia or Dystopia. The Utopians offer up their escapist dreams, while the Dystopians understand that the snake oil sold by the Utopia brokers will all come to ruin. The Utopians promise a future without want or need or fear or death, and yet which still exists within time; the Dystopians study history and extrapolate from past events to a future where the false gods have fallen once again. Already in 1960, Huston Smith delineated six tenets of the Utopian faith (although he did not delineate them as such), and they are worth recalling here because they are the recurring themes of terrestrial and extraterrestrial Utopias and Dystopias:

"First, we shall create life. ...

Second, we shall create minds. ...

Third, we shall created adjusted individuals via chemistry: tranquilizers and energizers, barbiturates and amphetamines, a complete pharmacopeia to control our moods and feelings.

Fourth, we shall create the good society via "behavioral engineering," a program of conditioning, liminal and subliminal, which through propaganda and hidden persuaders will induce men to behave in ways conducive to the commonweal.

Fifth, we shall create religious experiences by way of the psychedelics: LSD, mescaline, psilocybin, and their kin.

Sixth, we shall conquer death; achieve physical immortality by a combination of organ transplants and geriatrics that first arrest the aging process and then roll it back in rejuvenation. (Smith 187-8)

The lure of Utopia is very powerful, because each Utopian dream is born from the effort to escape what Mircea Eliade termed "the terror of history." Traditionally, man has lived in cyclical time, with mankind ritually returning to mythic time and events and framing the meaning of life in connection with events in the cycle of time, and mythic figures within that cycle. People were freed from profane time to live in connection with mythic time, relating their lives and cultures to a cycle of time vastly larger than themselves. In the words of Eliade, "In our opinion, only one fact counts: by virtue of this view, tens of millions of men were able, for century after century, to endure great historical pressures without despairing, without committing suicide or falling into that spiritual aridity that always brings with it a relativistic or nihilistic view of history." (Eliade 152) And this brings us back to despair. As Eliade observes, Judaism and Christianity have cyclical elements to religious observances, but are primarily linear in their approach to history; but with meaning and hope outside transcendent of, and giving meaning to, life within linear time. Utopianism fails because it attempts to create a state of perfection within present linear time Nihilism is the bitter fruit of every failed Utopia. In his insightful book on the topic of Utopia, Thomas Molnar observed as follows:

"... in reality, all utopians follow the same pattern: the liberation of man from *heteronomy*, from the guidance and providence of a personal God, in the name of *autonomy*, or moral self-government. But since this would lead immediately to anarchy, the emancipated individual is necessarily plunged by the utopian into the collectivity which will assume his guidance and provide for him. To realize the main objective of establishing an ideal community, the collectivity attempts to usurp the prerogatives and attributes proper to God. Such a collective divinity—an idol in the scriptural sense—will then lay claim to unchangeability, to what Raymond Ruyer refers as the maniacal will to continue the system guided and peopled by saints. The atheistic utopian does not mention God and heaven, except of course, as superstitious beliefs; he merely secularizes religious terminology, formulates a doctrine, devises ceremonies and recommends internal self-improvement and external conformity." (Molnar, 21)

Each of the six themes enunciated by Smith have been treated in fiction in Utopian or Dystopian terms. Utopia and Dystopia are the same thing, in the sense that Utopia is what is promised in the advertisements, and Dystopia is what actually shows up in the mail. Joined to various ideologies of Progress, both advocates and alarmist pontificating on the same themes speak in terms of an inevitability to that which was to come. O'Brien's words to Winston in George Orwell's novel, *1984* thus ring in the ears: "But always—do not forget this, Winston—always there will be the intoxication of power, constantly increasing and constantly growing subtler. Always, at every moment, there will be the thrill of victory, the sensation of trampling on an enemy who is helpless. If you want a picture of the

future, imagine a boot stamping on a human face—for ever.'"
Or, to again cite Molnar's analysis:

> At utopia's roots there is defiance of God, pride unlimited, a yearning for enormous power and the assumption of divine attributes with a view to manipulating and shaping mankind's fate. The utopian is not content with pressing men into a mould of his own manufacture; he is not a mere despot, dictator or totalitarian leader holding all temporal and spiritual power. His real vice is, first, the desire to dismantle human individuality through the dissolution of individual conscience and consciousness, and then to replace these with the collectivity and coalesced consciousness. ...
>
> What the utopian conceives of as the future, fabulous as it may seem is, in reality, a nightmare. It could not be otherwise because the utopian, in his speculation, ignores human nature, the rhythm of change, the fact that change involves not only gain but loss as well, the reality of time and the essential freedom of the soul. (Molnar, 227)

The pursuit of the exploration and settlement of the heavens has been permeated by a Utopian character from the beginning. As David Noble wrote in *The Religion of Technology:*

> In his great epic, *Orlando Furioso*, published in 1516, [Ludovico] Ariosto imagined a new means of escape from a fallen world. Astolfo, exploring the earth in a time of troubles, discovers the terrestrial paradise on a mountaintop. There he encounters St. John the Evangelist, who proposes that Astolfo continue on—"a flight more daring take, to yonder Moon." A century later, in 1611, the millenarian mystic Tommaso Campanella wrote to Galileo explaining how he had "read new meaning into

a familiar verse, 'and I saw a new Heaven and a new earth,'—namely, that the moon and the planets were inhabited." In his later *Apologia pro Galileo* he suggested the possibility that paradise was not really terrestrial at all, but lay on the moon, which was situated high enough above the earth to have been spared the deluge of the flood. The moon must have a moderate climate, Campanella argued, because its Edenic inhabitants, "not infected with Adam's sin," went naked. (Noble 115–6)

The *Star Trek* universe (at least as originally conceived), in which poverty, crime, racism, want and need had been eliminated (fortunately warfare with the less-enlightened still existed, or the show would have been as interesting as a Soviet crop report) offers a modern example of the same mentality, in secularized form. On the one hand, we are promised a paradise among the stars (new technologies, vast wealth, limitless energy, room to expand); on the other hand, we are threatened with death if we remain on earth ("all our eggs in one basket," AIDS, killer comets, etc.). All dressed up in seemingly-secular attire, those who seek to "immanentize the eschaton"— to create their version of a heaven on Earth, or Mars— have nearly trapped the exploration and settlement of new worlds between Scylla of impossible expectations, and the Charybdis of irrational fears. And a population, suitably numbed by conveniences and chemicals, soma and satellite television, has little interest in the costs and risks of a space program that is no where near as cheap or interesting as a CGI *War and Peace* in the heavens told in forty-four minutes, or less.

Raised on a diet of determinism and nihilistic materialism, cut off from the past and without a thought for the future, men who once dreamed of being gods are taught to doubt whether they are really even self-aware. And history—impersonal and unstoppable—has become the implacable foe of stability and even survival. In the words of Eliade, "modern man's boasted freedom to make history is illusory for nearly the whole of the human race. At most, man is left free to choose between two positions: (1) to oppose the history that is being made by the very small minority (and, in this case, he is free to choose between suicide and deportation); (2) to take refuge in a subhuman existence or in flight." (Eliade 156-7) Deportation and refuge in flight have, of course, both been set forth as Dystopian and Utopian motivations for space settlement. But it is most important that we understand Eliade's point. This is the terror of history in which modern humanity is immersed: a nihilism in which the thousand masks of "Progress" drop to reveal the face of a determinism without a *telos*, the unbearable sense of personal awareness bound to a self-negating, yet dominant, ideology which insists that this very self-awareness is a biochemical illusion. Thus Man must inevitably kill himself if his assault on meaning is anything other than vain posing. Far from being the birth of the *übermensch,* the 'death of God' is the death of man.

In the face of the present *fear* which drives some, the *despair* which holds back others, and the *doubt* which pervades throughout, we turn to the Virtues. Our *techne* is not lacking—we have many clever craftsmen. We are masters of deracinated facts which have been uprooted from connection to the Truth—but how shall the branches endure without the Vine?

Techne is an expression of what is *in* man whether in accumulation of facts, in technical expertise, or in formulation of 'ethical guidelines'; what is needed for community is that which transcends humanity, including the source of the Virtues and love of the Truth. As John Haught observed in his recent book, *Is Nature Enough?*,

As long as one maintains that moral ideals can be accounted for ultimately in a purely natural— and that means an evolutionary— way, they can be neither lofty nor ideal. ...

... Moreover, if evolutionary, social and historical factors were fully determinative of my actions, then there would be no point in talking about ethics or morality at all. Without the assumption of freedom, ethics could be replaced completely by disciplines that describe and explain behavior in terms of inviolable constants and laws of nature. (Haught 148, 154)

The love of the Truth—theological truth, intellectual truth, moral truth —is the font of the Virtues. The Virtues—or their lack—determine how mankind will make use of his technologies; ethics disconnected from Virtue descend simply to the level of arbitrary rules.

Technology is, in essence, morally neutral. The demonization of technical knowledge precisely *misses* the target by *avoiding* the real problem. If we are afraid of our technologies, it is because we are (rightly) afraid of ourselves; if we are not afraid of ourselves, then our cause for fear should be all the greater because it bespeaks a lack of introspection.

There are some who believe the fear of extinction should move us to the stars; this is the point where the "killer asteroid/comet" comes into play, combined with a quick wave of the hands and invocation of the 'fact' of 'statistical certainty.' The 'statistical certainty' that such prognostications do not take into account is that the same technologies which would avert such a disaster can also be turned to cause it. "Mass drivers" are simply another escalation in our capacity for killing each other. We cannot engineer our way out of the darkness which resides within the hearts of men. We cannot flee that which would accompany us wherever we would go. The light of hope must enter and dispel the darkness.

There are some who believe that the promise of a boundless paradise of material prosperity should move us to the stars; but the almost unimaginable increase in wealth in the past several thousand years has not demonstrably made us happier or more virtuous. Arguably, we have more prosperity right now than we know what to do with, and there are few who see why anything should interrupt their fun so that future generations can enjoy more of the same. More material goods, more accumulation of facts cannot fill the emptiness of the soul which has lost its way. The fellowship of souls united in hope which is the essence of community is what is lacking.

Human exploration and settlement is, at its very heart, a story of community, and where there is community, there is the opportunity for the exercise of the virtues as a necessary component of a thriving civilization. Virtue upholds a civilization, Virtue binds together a healthy community. *Human history readily demonstrates that people can live without prosperity or peace; they can endure through plague and poverty, slavery and concentration camps, but they cannot live without hope*. St. Paul wrote, "For I consider that the sufferings of this present time are not worthy *to be compared* with the glory which shall be revealed in us. For the earnest expectation of the creation eagerly waits for the revealing of the sons of God. For the creation was subjected to futility, not willingly, but because of Him who subjected *it* in hope; because the creation itself also will be delivered from the bondage of corruption into the glorious liberty of the children of God." (Romans 8:18–21)

People can endure the horrible wickedness done because of hate and fear, if they are sustained by love. In the words of St. John, "There is no fear in love; but perfect love casts out fear, because fear involves torment. But he who fears has not been made perfect in love." (1 John 4:18) And as St. Paul wrote, "Love suffers long *and* is kind; love does not envy; love does not parade itself, is not puffed up; does not behave rudely, does not seek its own, is not provoked, thinks no evil; does not rejoice in iniquity, but rejoices in the truth; bears all things, believes all things, hopes all things, endures all things." (1 Corinthians 13:4–7)

A community can survive betrayal, hypocrisy, and all of man's failures to live up to that which Virtue teaches, if it does not lose faith. As St. Paul wrote to the Church in Rome: "For we were saved in this hope, but hope that is seen is not hope; for why does one still hope for what he sees? But if we hope for what we do not see, we eagerly wait for *it* with perseverance." (Romans 8:24–25)

Such transcendent faith, hope and love cannot be overcome—not even by the death of the flesh. The great martyrs of old—men such as St. Ignatius of Antioch or St. Laurence of Rome—provide exceptional examples, for they sought not to impose their beliefs on anyone, but were willing to bear witness to the faith, hope and love that lived within them, even at the cost of their lives. You can slay such a person, but you cannot truly kill him, and his example strengthens the entire community.

In the midst of his famous speech of September 12, 1962, President John F. Kennedy noted that "William Bradford, speaking in 1630 of the founding of the Plymouth Bay Colony, said that all great and honorable actions are accompanied with great difficulties, and both must be enterprised and overcome with answerable courage."[12] President Kennedy understood the application of those words to the dawning "Space Race" of his time, and it is not hard to see their applicability to our hopes, as well. Faith, Hope and Love support and sustain the other virtues,

---

[12] http://www.historyplace.com/speeches/jfk-space.htm (referenced August 6, 2008)

such as courage, and the willingness to defer our own gratification for the sake of our neighbors, and future generations.

It has long been observed that the Christian lives as a citizen of two kingdoms—one in this world, and the other both now, and after this world—and for him there is no contradiction between an awareness of the limits of man—and the finite span of his days—and an active, meaningful life in the present. It means living in the awareness that all human civilizations are transient; "For here we have no continuing city, but we seek the one to come," as the writer to the Hebrews declares in the fourth chapter. The awareness that this world is passing away is not a reason to despair, but a spur to use one's time and abilities to the glory of the Creator. As St. Peter wrote:

> Therefore, since all these things will be dissolved, what manner of persons ought you to be in holy conduct and godliness, looking for and hastening the coming of the day of God, because of which the heavens will be dissolved, being on fire, and the elements will melt with fervent heat? Nevertheless we, according to His promise, look for new heavens and a new earth in which righteousness dwells. (2 Peter 3:11–13)

The exercise of the Virtues is seeking and doing that which is noble in the face of all that which would deny the very existence of Truth and Virtue—to keep faith when others mock; to show courage in defense of Truth, when everyone else counsels running away to save your own hide; to love your neighbor as yourself, even to the point of laying down your life for your friends—this is pursuit of Virtue which must be at the heart of a living civilization—and living civilizations thrive on challenges. They create great art and music and literature, examine the hearts of men and explore their frontiers.

Such life comes from Hope, and Hope is born of the Word of Truth. In our age's obsession with *techne*, we have often forgotten the power of the *logos*, the power of the Word. One of our age's greatest servants of the Word was recently taken from us, and although this is not the time or place, perhaps, for an extended reflection upon the life and work of Alexander Solzhenitsyn, there are words in his *Nobel Lecture* which are quite germane to our topic today. He confronted the danger of despair which grew in the face of the brutality and violence which attended the failure of a materialistic form of Utopianism, and he proclaimed that its might would be broken through the Hope born of the Word.

  We shall be told: What can literature do in the face of a remorseless assault of open violence? But let us not forget that violence does not and cannot exist by itself: It is invariably intertwined with *the lie*. ... The simple act of an ordinary brave man is not to participate in lies, not to support false actions! His rule: let *that* come into the world, let it even reign supreme— only not through me. But it is within the power of writers and artists to do much more: *to defeat the lie!* ...

  The favorite proverbs in Russian are about *truth*. They forcefully express a long and difficult national experience, sometimes in striking fashion:

One word of truth shall outweigh the whole world.

  It is on such a seemingly fantastic violation of the law of conservation of mass and energy that my own activity is based, and my appeal to the writers of the world. (Solzhenitsyn 526)

For too long, the mirages of the Utopians have led so many to the death of hope; many have succumbed to the lie, and fallen into despair. We do not seek to 'immanentize the eschaton,' but to recognize that our lives in time are flawed and brief, but in their midst there remains the possibility of hope because the Creator of all was not only transcendent but also immanent, and did not despise what He had made; but in the incarnation, the eternal *Logos*, the Word of God "made Himself of no reputation, taking the form of a bondservant, and coming in the likeness of men. And being found in appearance as a man, He humbled Himself and became obedient to the point of death, even the death of the cross." (Phil. 2:7–8)

We do not seek Utopia; we seek to live, and to live nobly. "The settling of the Martian New World is an opportunity for a noble experiment in which humanity has another chance to shed old baggage and begin the world anew; carrying forward as much of the best of our heritage as possible and leaving the worst behind. Such chances do not come often, and are not to be disdained lightly." Such shedding of old baggage and beginning anew, we call metanoia, repentance, and truly it is not to be disdained lightly. We cannot change the things that we have done, but we can begin anew. The Truth has such power, establishing and sustaining the Virtues, overturning despair and building up Hope through the Word of Truth, casting aside hatred through Love, and dispelling doubt through Faith. We can begin anew, restored to our place among the generations, building a future for the generations to follow until our course is run, all the while as pilgrim people passing through this brief life, trusting in the One who establishes and sustains. "For I consider that the sufferings of this present time are not worthy *to be compared* with the glory which shall be revealed in us. For the earnest expectation of the creation eagerly waits for the revealing of the sons of God. For the creation was subjected to futility, not willingly, but because of Him who subjected *it* in hope; because the creation itself also will be delivered from the bondage of corruption into the glorious liberty of the children of God." (Romans 8:18–21)

Works Cited:

Eliade, Mircea, *The Myth of the Eternal Return* (Princeton & Oxford: Princeton University Press, 2005)

Haught, John, *Is Nature Enough?* (Cambridge: Cambridge University Press, 2006)

Lukacs, John, *At the End of an Age* (New Haven & London: Yale University Press, 2002)

Molnar, Thomas, *Utopia, the Perennial Heresy* (New York: Sheed and Ward, 1967)

Noble, David, *The Religion of Technology* (New York: Penguin, 1999)

Porpora, Douglas, *Landscapes of the Soul, the Loss of Moral Meaning in American Life* (Oxford, 2001)

Smith, Houston, *Beyond the Post-Modern Mind* (New York: Crossroads, 1982)

Solzhenitsyn, Alexander, *The Solzhenitsyn Reader— New and Essential Writings 1947–2005*, ed. by Edward E. Ericson, Jr. and Daniel J. Mahoney (Wilmington: ISI Books, 2006)

IV. "Faith and Community: Moving Beyond LEO"[13]

Abstract:

In an age centered on personal security and affluence, what could motivate a civilization to expand beyond low Earth orbit and open another chapter in the history of humanity? Political elites pursue agendas dominated by shortsighted ambition, and hypothetical financial gains beyond LEO have a hard time competing with far more certain, if mundane, terrestrial investments. The drive for our species to move beyond its current sphere could certainly provide tangible benefits in keeping with the desires of the elites, but such benefits do not constitute a sufficient motivation. Human exploration and settlement is a story of community, and where there is community, there is the opportunity for the exercise of the virtues necessary for a thriving civilization.

Dreaming of a New World

In the main, those of us who have gathered for the thirteenth annual international Mars Society convention have come to this place in pursuit of a dream. We give attention to the words of those men and women who have devoted their lives to a wide array of scientific endeavors, and we give some time to the opining and posturing of *homo politicus*, and perhaps even attend to a few words from historians and other students of letters. But we do so in pursuit of a dream.

The dream which animates the Mars Society is set forth in the Founding Declaration, which declares, among other points:

We must go for the opportunity. The settling of the Martian New World is an opportunity for a noble experiment in which humanity has another chance to shed old baggage and begin the world anew; carrying for-

---

[13] This essay was presented to the thirteenth annual international convention of the Mars Society, meeting in Dayton, Ohio in August 2010.

ward as much of the best of our heritage as possible and leaving the worst behind. Such chances do not come often, and are not to be disdained lightly.[14]

Mars is seen as a "new world" and "another chance" at attaining a place most rare: Somewhere to "begin the world anew". The dream is declared unflinchingly in this Founding Declaration—quite possibly in ignorance of its boldness, because to dream of a new world is an astoundingly audacious act. One might say that a leap into the dark is inextricably connected to any such dream, a leap seemingly irrational, given a moment's reflection. If some of the great minds of the modern scientific age have marveled that the most incomprehensible thing about the universe is that it is comprehensible, what might one say about the act of trying to render comprehensible—and ultimately corporeal—that which has no existence outside the mind? Because the "new world" of Mars will only exist in such a fashion for the immediate future.

To dream of a new world is more than simply to postulate the uncovering of some undiscovered aspect of our own world; ancient tales of discovery are replete with such explorations which unveil a previously hidden corner of our world. In fact, the dream of a new world has a closer kinship to the accounts of journeys which revealed a world concealed within

---

[14] http://www.marssociety.org/portal/groups/tmssc/founding_declaration

our own—one which is unattainable apart from a special grace granted to the traveler.[15]

The dream of the new world is not merely a voyage of discovery; it includes, but is not encompassed by, a discovery of the physical facts of the red planet and the means for the practical utilization of those resources for the benefit of human existence. A new world is something akin to a new home. A home does not reduce to its parts: It is not simply a matter of a quantity of wood, nails, sheetrock, paint, an assortment of electrical fixtures, and the rest of an itemized inventory, assembled according to the principles of civil engineering. Instead, a home is a complex interaction of human activity by those who are bound together by rite and by blood in the midst of such an environment, and that home cannot be utterly extracted from its larger environment—and attendant human community—without, once again, simply reducing it to an abstraction.

The dream of a new world has slowly, steadily emerged over the course of the past seven centuries, an unanticipated consequence of rattling, and finally breaking, of certain fetters imposed upon the Western mind by Aristotelean thought. For the most part, Aristotle's views were readily accepted at the heart of the curriculum of the medieval universities. But Aristotle had excluded the possibility of the existence of more than one world as a logical impossibility, and thus the action of Eti-

---

[15] Thus, for example, when St. Brendan and his monks, near the conclusion of the *Navagatio*, are granted the attainment of their goal—to visit the Island of Promise—it is with the understanding that they may not remain. "He turned to Brendan. 'Now, at last, you have found the land you have been seeking all these years. The Lord Jesus Christ did not allow you to find it immediately, because first He wished to show you the richness of His wonders in the deep. Fill your ship brim-full with precious stones and return to the land of your birth. The day of your final journey is at hand; you shall soon be laid to rest with your fathers. After many more years have rolled by, this land will be revealed to your successors at the time when Christians will be undergoing persecution." (*The Age of Bede* 267)

enne Tempier, bishop of Paris, in 1277 through the condemnation of 219 propositions drawn from Aristotelean doctrine, allowed for a range of speculation which threw open the shutters on the Western mind. When that peculiar institution born of the Middle Ages—the University[16]—arose in twelfth century Europe, the translations of Greek and Arabic sources brought a flood of ancient thought into the brightest minds of the rising generation. Aristotle's contributions to ethics and philosophy were quite profound, but his influence on natural science could have held back the rise of the sciences indefinitely if not for the Condemnations of 1277. As Edward Grant wrote in *The Foundations of Modern Science in the Middle Ages*, "By emphasizing God's absolute power to do anything short of a logical contradiction, the articles condemned in 1277 had a curious, and probably unintended, effect: they encouraged speculation about natural impossibilities in the Aristotelean world system, which were often treated as hypothetical possibilities." (Grant 81)

The freedom to speculate in ways which ran counter to Aristotle's system brought with it the notion that more than one world could exist. Again, in the words of Grant:

> The possibility that matter might exist beyond our world in the form of other worlds became a major subject of discussion as a result of the Condemnation of 1277. ... The Condemnation of 1277 dramatically altered the intellectual context at the University of Paris, and after 1277, the question about other worlds became commonplace. Article 34 was condemned because it denied that God could make more than one world.

---

[16] Grant highlights the unique character of the development of the university: "From the earliest societies of ancient Egypt and Mesopotamia, numerous diverse urban civilizations had come and gone, but none had produced anything comparable to the universities of Europe." (Grant 34)

Thereafter, all had to concede that God could create as many other worlds as he pleased. (Grant 120)

The conceptual breakthrough left intact the doctrine of the uniformity of physical laws—but those laws would now apply to each world.[17]

The vital spark to the imagination which came in 1277 not only allowed for consideration of the planets as worlds; it open a path to thinking of such worlds as homes to their own inhabitants, and possible destinations for human exploration. Each world was thought of as existing at the center of its own conceptual system, and each would conform to the universal laws of nature.[18] The way was opened to thus think of the planets of the solar system as worlds unto themselves, and conceived of in such terms, the imagination of man began to populate such "new worlds" with people fitting to them. For example, Johannes Kepler's 1634 *Somnium*—or *Dream*[19]—envisioned not only a trip to the moon, and the astronomical perspective afforded from that vantage point, but also speculated concerning the nature of the lunar inhabitants, whom he divided into Subvolvians (the near side inhabitants) and Privolvians (on the far side). (Dick 77–78) But then, Nicholas of Cusa (1401–1464)—one of the most influential cardinals of the early

---

[17] "Following the Condemnation of 1277, many deemed what was impossible in Aristotle's natural philosophy to be possible and plausible. Aristotle's physics and cosmology could operate in numerous worlds, if God chose to create those worlds." (Grant 121)

[18] Grant concurs: "During the Middle Ages, there were no actual supporters of the existence of other worlds. It was apparently sufficient to demonstrate that if God made other world—and it was always conceded that he could do so—they would be subject to the same physical laws as our world." (121)

[19] Thus we might say that Kepler, too, understood the dreamlike character of all such imaginings.

fifteen century—had already indulged in such speculations several centuries earlier. As John Wilkins' cited Nicholas in his 1638 book, *A World in the Moon*:

> We may conjecture (saith he) the inhabiters of the Sun are like to the nature of that Planet, more clear and bright, more intellectual and spiritual than those in the Moon where they are nearer to the nature of that duller Planet, and those of the earth being more gross and material than either, so that these intellectual natures in the Sun, are more form than matter, those in the earth more matter than form, and those in the Moon betwixt both. ... In some such manner likewise it is with the regions of the other Stars, for we conjecture that none of them are without inhabitants, but that there are so many particular worlds and parts of this one universe, as there are Stars which are innumerable, unless it be to Him who created all things in number. (Wilkins 194–5)

Once the deadlock of the Aristotelean system had been broken by the doctrine of divine omnipotence, speculations concerning the character of new worlds (and their inhabitants) was but a continued development of the theme. But the next, and crucial, step was to conceive of those inhabitants as human beings who had crossed the void—men and women who would not only transport themselves to these new worlds, but would even imagine that they would transform these worlds according to their own designs.

Thinking upon a New Civilization

But when we think of expanding human civilization to a new world, Mars, we are actually doing more than imagining a new world. Dreaming of a new world was a breakthrough in human thought, but in a sense the consideration of the creation of a new civilization *should* be no less amazing. Considerations of the shape of such new civilizations have been the focus of some of the best (and worst) literary efforts of the past century. The thought experiments of speculative fiction have produced seemingly innumerable ranks of imaginary civilizations, usually built around the complex interaction of elements of continuity and creativity from the old world to the new. A significant theme of such speculations has been that we cannot, or will not, escape who we have been, and what we have done, and even though we exchange one world for another, such future civilizations will remain comprehensible. According to the words of Ecclesiastes,

That which has been *is* what will be,
That which *is* done is what will be done,
And *there is* nothing new under the sun.
Is there anything of which it may be said,
"See, this *is* new"?
It has already been in ancient times before us.
There is no remembrance of former *things,*
Nor will there be any remembrance of *things* that are to come
By *those* who will come after. (1:9–11)

The technologies of different ages and cultures change, but the imagined future of humanity remains comprehensible and varies less than some might imagine—or hope.

But while the modern age brought with it the capacity to dream of new worlds, the same age has left many of its children less capable of understanding the nature of the humanity that might inhabit such worlds. Our age has brought forth great advances in *techné*—in craftsmanship, if you will—so that our technology vastly expands our ability to gather facts far beyond the natural limitations of bodily sensation. But our age has just as often left us epistemologically impoverished with regards to the necessary integration of such data with that which was once known, and now has largely been forgotten, from other fields of knowledge. That is to say, while we have generated a vast array of knowledge in various fields of natural science, we have neglected history, humane letters, political philosophy—or, even worse, such forms of knowledge have been supplanted by ideological constructs—a species of what was once called "the profane *and* idle babblings and contradictions of what is falsely called knowledge" (1 Tim. 6:20 NKJV). *Thus an age which may have the technological capacity to establish a civilization on a new world lacks the knowledge which underpins civilization.* Russell Kirk well described our ideological age,

> To resume, nevertheless the typical ideologue thinks of himself as perfectly objective. The core of his belief is that human nature and human society may be improved infinitely—nay, perfected—by the application of the techniques of the physical and biological sciences to the governance of men. Nearly all nineteenth and twentieth-century radical movements drew their inspiration in considerable part from this positivistic assumption; Marxism is only one of the more systematic products of this view of life and thought. For the convinced positivist-ideologue, traditional religion has been a nuisance and a curse, because it impedes the designs of the ideological planner. Science, with a Roman S, should supplant God. The religious teacher would give way to the "scientific" manager of the new society.
>
> This rather vague claim that society ought to be regulated on "scientific" principles has held an appeal for some physical and biological scientists; and the less such scientists have known of humane letters, history,

and political theory, the more enthusiastic they have tended to be for a new order which would sweep away all the errors and follies of mankind by a radical application of scientific theory and method. The high achievements of physical and biological sciences in the nineteenth century gave powerful reinforcement to advocates of "scientism" in sociology and politics. Religion, moral tradition, and the complex of established political institutions were irrational and unscientific and subjective, it seemed; surely the scientists must show the preachers and politicians the way to a better world.

Earlier, the establishment of a new world was likened to a new home, and it was observed that a home is a complex interaction of human activity by those who are bound together by rite and by blood in the midst of such an environment. A civilization is bound together not only by a shared territory, but also by much more than merely location, for the families which make up that civilization share a culture with a common history, defined body of received law, and public and private rites relating to virtually every aspect of life. These public and private rites are informed by the other elements of culture and they, in turn, reinforce, and give expression to, the civilization as a whole. In short, civilizational concerns are often preeminent concerns for humanity, and our age's seeming inability to understand this is not a negation of the significance of culture, but a symptom of our current degraded condition. Thus Chantal Delsol wrote in *Icarus Fallen*:

> For the past two centuries, in order to escape from the labyrinth of mediocrity, we have believed ourselves capable of radically transforming man and society. Since Condorcet, the philosophy of Progress has promised to eliminate war, disease, and need, and various ideologies

have announced a radiant future. We have just come to the realization—because of the revelation of human disasters in Eastern Europe, and in the West through the reappearance of poverty, illiteracy, war, and epidemics—that these hopes were finally in vain. We have fallen back to earth, where we must re-appropriate our human condition. But along the way we have lost the keys of understanding, and we no longer realize this mediocre world, nor do we know its meaning. (xxiii–xxiv)

The solutions to our most pressing problems are not technological. Human civilizations are not engineered; in fact, attempts at social engineering have consistently led to debacle or disaster, with the ruinous ends of such endeavors being proportional to the grandiosity of the theory which propelled such schemes in the first place. The utopian phantasm of engineering a perfect society should have shared the tumbrel ride with Robespierre in 1794, but the self-deification of his imitators (conscious or otherwise) has continued to the present.

In the assessment of Delsol, civilization cannot be engineered, and the attempt to execute such an endeavor may weaken, or even kill, the civilization which does, in fact, exist. Actually, Delsol asserts that we have come to precisely such an end:

Western man at the beginning of the twenty-first century is the descendant of Icarus. He wonders into what world he has fallen. It is as if someone has thrown him into a game without giving him the rules. When he asks around for instructions, he is invariably told that they have been lost. He is amazed that everyone is content to live in a world without meaning and without identity, where no one seems to know either why he lives or why he dies. (xxiv)

Such disorientation is only to be expected for men and women who have become, in essence, uncivilized. Uprooted modern humanity suffers from a disorientation similar to that of a man who, when he asked for a map of Chicago or Calcutta—or any other place marked by life in the real world—was handed instead an image of Campanella's "City of the Sun." Such a place does not, and cannot, exist and one will remain lost as long as he attempts to navigate the 'city of man' according to such a design.

The succession of such schemes has left behind men and women who have despaired of any order and purpose in life; they have, in effect, become uncivilized. They have disavowed either loyalty or relation to the broader community of what was a common people. They will neither acknowledge their ancestors nor provide a fitting inheritance for their descendants in maintaining the continuity of that which must be the permanent things. They have, in short, become what Edmund Burke foresaw in 1790 regarding the effects of a deterioration of the bedrock of civilization:

> But one of the first and most leading principles on which the commonwealth and the laws are consecrated, is lest the temporary possessors and life-renters in it, unmindful of what they have received from their ancestors, or of what is due to their posterity, should act as if they were the entire masters; that they should not think it among their rights to cut off the entail, or commit waste on the inheritance, by destroying at their pleasure the whole original fabric of their society; hazarding to leave to those who come after them a ruin instead of an habitation—and teaching these successors as little to respect their contrivances, as they had themselves respected the institutions of their forefathers. By this unprincipled facility of changing the state as often, and as much, and in as many ways, as there are floating fan-

cies or fashions, the whole chain and continuity of the commonwealth would be broken. No one generation could link with the other. Men would become little better than the flies of a summer. (95)

Apart from the indispensable elements of civilization—a shared culture, common history, law, and rites—there is the belief, rooted in the history of the origins of any given civilization, that a theophanic event shaped its beginning. Such a perceived theophany establishes the dream of the civilization; its "dream" is believed to not originate with man, but from God. The quintessential examples within the context of Western civilization of such theophanies are those given to Abraham and Moses. Thus we hear concerning Abraham in Genesis 12: "Now the LORD had said to Abram: 'Get out of your country, from your family and from your father's house, to a land that I will show you. I will make you a great nation; I will bless you and make your name great; and you shall be a blessing. I will bless those who bless you, and I will curse him who curses you; and in you all the families of the earth shall be blessed.'" (v. 1–3 NKJV) The divine command to depart from one land to another is combined with a promise of a blessing not only to the individual, but to a civilization which begins in him; in time, by divine decree, even the patriarch's name is changed from Abram ("Exalted Father") to Abraham ("Father of a Multitude"), so that in his very name the relationship of Abraham to all who would be descended of his faith was given clear expression. In the case of Moses, the first theophany—the burning bush (Exodus 3–4)—is connected to the fulfillment of the earlier revelation to Abraham, so that the call of Abraham and the word given to Moses are joined together in the foundation of a faith linked to a promised place. And later theophanies, such as at the baptism of Jesus, would proclaim that the promise of the place was fulfilled.

Other civilizations point to a divine protection extended to their founders. For example, Plutarch famously relates that a sign of divine favor was manifested in the care of the infants Romulus and Remus, who were kept alive by a she-wolf and woodpecker; "these creatures," Plutarch declares, "are esteemed holy to the god Mars; the woodpecker the Latins still especially worship and honor." (27) The location of Rome was entrusted to divination: "Concluding at last to decide the contest by divination from a flight of birds... Hence it is that the Romans, in their divination from birds, chiefly regard the vulture..." (31)

However, there is little point to multiplying such examples, because they are extremely widespread—certainly the foundations of the New England colonies were not lacking in assertions of providential care, and such testimonies were regularly linked implicitly or explicitly to those found within the Old and New Testament. The point which is being made here is simply the assertion that both for the founders of a given civilization and for their 'descendants' a sense of divine establishment gives shape to the resultant people. The place, foundational figures, fundamental traditions, law and religious beliefs are all connected with a perception of divine guidance or divine favor in the establishing of the various civilizations. At such a momentous time as the beginning of a new stage in human history and civilization, that which has come before is expanded, purified, adapted to a new context. There is a vital continuity which finds new expression, but also elements which are undeniably new, and which will be of profound significance for succeeding generations.

Regardless of whether one would believe such accounts or not, it seems clear that many of the founders of various civilizations did believe them, and attempts to *artificially* establish such foundational myths have utterly failed. Auguste Comte's Positivism, as well as the myths of Vladimir Lenin, Joseph Stalin, and Adolf Hitler, all represent readily perceived perversions of the foundational myth; being readily recognized as contrived, their appeal was short-lived, albeit horrifically dangerous during their duration. Indeed, the appeal of such cults of personality in the modern age may have arisen precisely because of the modern disconnection from the received cultures of past generations. Being unrooted, the children of modernity have flailed around looking for a past which they might contrive for themselves so that they could have some sense of identity. They are lacking a theophanic event to which they perceive a relation by blood or tradition or doctrine. It is thus that the children of modernity have, in essence, raised up idols, and the sacrifices which were often made to such idols have been terrible—and reached their worst precisely when the objects of idolatry proclaimed that there was no authority higher than man. Thus one reads in St. Paul's words in Romans 1:

> The wrath of God is being revealed from heaven against all the godlessness and wickedness of men who suppress the truth by their wickedness, since what may be known about God is plain to them, because God has made it plain to them. For since the creation of the world God's invisible qualities—his eternal power and divine nature—have been clearly seen, being understood from what has been made, so that men are without excuse. For although they knew God, they neither glorified him as God nor gave thanks to him, but their thinking became futile and their foolish hearts were darkened. Although they claimed to be wise, they became fools 23and exchanged the glory of the immortal

God for images made to look like mortal man and birds and animals and reptiles. (v. 18–22)

Furthermore, since they did not think it worthwhile to retain the knowledge of God, he gave them over to a depraved mind, to do what ought not to be done. They have become filled with every kind of wickedness, evil, greed and depravity. They are full of envy, murder, strife, deceit and malice. They are gossips, slanderers, God-haters, insolent, arrogant and boastful; they invent ways of doing evil; they disobey their parents; they are senseless, faithless, heartless, ruthless. Although they know God's righteous decree that those who do such things deserve death, they not only continue to do these very things but also approve of those who practice them. (v. 28–32)

A civilization must be perceived to be established on the basis of truth for the advancement of that truth; but now the post-modern confusion advances a dogma which, in flagrant self-contradiction, admits no challenge: All truth is relative; what is true for one person is not necessarily true for another. The logical and philosophical incoherence of such an assertion aside, the immediate effect of such a belief is the atomizing of society into self-centered units who care nothing for the preservation of their own civilization[20] and the preservation of the most fundamental units of civilization found in hearth and home. In such a relativized condition, the power of the governing authorities is arbitrary and absolute: Owing no loyalty to divinity or fixed law, the relationship of governing to governed is unmediated by inherited, and mutual, obligations. John Haught well-summarizes the dilemma of our time:

---

[20] In fact, such individuals may take umbrage at the idea that they are in fact the inheritors of a civilization.

If we really believed that truth is merely a human construct, then the pursuit of truth could no longer function to give purpose or meaning to our lives. To experience meaning in life, after all, requires the humble submission of our minds and lives to a value that pulls us out of ourselves and gives us something noble to live for. It entails a commitment to something greater than ourselves. Having a sense of meaning is the consequence of *being grasped* by a value or values that we did not invent and that will outlive us. If we sincerely thought that we were the sole creators of truth then truth could no longer function to give purpose to our lives, nor would it allow our intelligence to function critically. If evolutionary naturalists *consistently* thought that truth—along with other values—were nothing more than the products of genes, minds, or cultures, then such a fabrication could no longer function to give meaning to their own lives either.

For a value to be the source of meaning it has to function as more than an arbitrary human invention. If I thought of truth as the product of human creativity alone, then there would be nothing to prevent me from deciding that deception rather than truth-telling should guide my life and actions. (Haught 103)

Thus our post-modern dilemma. As John Carroll observes near the end of his recent book, *The Wreck of Western Culture—Humanism Revisited*, "A society cannot survive which is so fragmented that, at best, it contains a few individuals with intellectual integrity, while the rest go about their profane routines." (229) Mankind cannot endure an imagined 'end of history' wherein the goal of life is simply satiety. Such a fate is a living death.

Prospects for a New Civilization on a New World

As stated previously, *we live in an age which may have the technological capacity to establish a civilization on a new world but which lacks the knowledge which underpins civilization.* Neither public policy, nor corporate decisions, in the main, are inclined to address this dilemma. Civilizational concerns are too 'big picture' for those inclined to simply treat the symptoms, rather than the disease, which afflicts post-modernity.

What is needed is to confront the 'new frontier' in civilizational terms. To cast the opening of a new world in terms of scientific and financial benefits misses that which is of far greater weight at this time. There is little public support for, or interest in, an Antarctic-style "ant farm" of scientists pursuing doctoral theses on topics perceived to be far removed from the interests and concerns of the people who are expected to pay the bills. In fact, if such endeavors are going to gain public support, it can only be by demonstrating a readily perceptible benefit to the entire civilization.

So, too, the appeal to hypothetical profits is real, but probably insufficient to establish a new civilization on a new world. To state it crassly, smart investors look for a sure, if small, return—not investments which are easily perceived to be extremely risky. Most of those entrepreneurs who have invested in "space" have done so because a personal (and quite commendable) commitment. But despite such substantial commitments, it is far from certain that such efforts will take humanity beyond LEO for the foreseeable future. Even if "space tourism" economic models do prove to be financially rewarding, it is a long way (in every sense of those words) from there to establishing a new branch of human civilization on another world.

For now, the path to a new civilization on a new world is uncertain, at best, because it is not simply a matter of technological considerations. We are slow to expand into new frontiers—which would then open up new branches of human civilization—because our own civilization is, to put it bluntly, broken. Civilization gives rise to civilization, as what has been enters a wilderness and is reshaped in ways which cannot be entirely anticipated in advance. For now, what is needed is to fan the embers of what little remains if we want to have a legacy which can be the 'seed stock' of any future civilization. Whatever shape a future civilization might take on another world, it seems certain that it will be both very much like what has come before, and yet renewed in ways which cannot yet be entirely anticipated—and certainly not planned. But that which may take root and spring up in the midst of a most distant desert may help to revitalize our weary world, as well.

–S.D.G.—

Works Cited:

[anon.] "The Voyage of St Brendan," in *The Age of Bede*, trans. by J. F. Webb, ed. by D. H. Farmer, (New York: Penguin, 1965)

Burke, Edmund, *Reflections on the Revolution in France*, (Oxford: Oxford University Press, 1993)

Carroll, John, *The Wreck of Western Culture—Humanism Revisited*, (Wilmington, Delaware: ISI Books, 2008)

Delsol, Chantal, *Icarus Fallen—The Search for Meaning in an Uncertain World*, trans. by Robin Dick (Wilmington, Delaware: ISI Books, 2003)

Dick, Steven J., *Plurality of Worlds—The Origins of the Extraterrestrial Life Debate from Democritus to Kant* ((Cambridge: Cambridge University Press, 1984)

Grant, Edward, *The Foundations of Modern Science in the Middle Ages*, (Cambridge: Cambridge University Press, 1996)

Haught, John, *Is Nature Enough?—Meaning and Truth in the Age of Science,* (Cambridge: Cambridge University Press, 2006)

Kirk, Russell, "The Drug of Ideology," in *The Essential Russell Kirk*, (Wilmington, Delaware: ISI Books, 2007)

Plutarch's Lives, ed. by Arthur Hugh Clough, vol. 1 (New York: The Modern Library, 2001)

Wilkins, John, *The Discovery of a World in the Moone, or, a Discourse tending to Prove, that 'tis probable there may be another habitable World in that Planet*, (London: Michael Sparl and Edward Forrest, 1638). Reprinted in facsimile in 1972 by Theatrum Orbis Terrarum Ltd., Amsterdam.

Made in the USA
Charleston, SC
01 May 2011